Cowgirl Skirts and Music Boxes

Poetry by Judy Shimek Drechsler

2017
Falling into One a book of poetry

"The Garden in Winter" *Oasis Journal 2017*

2018
"Cowgirl Skirts and Music Boxes" *Oasis Journal 2018*

Ars Poetica Juried Art/Poetry Show "where art and poetry meet" poems chosen to be illustrated by artists: 2018-2019
- "walking in Nuremberg after a fall rain" artist: Joanne Schoener Scott, Front Street Gallery
- "When My Husband Died" artist: Sarah June Steffen, Poulsbohemian Coffeehose

2019
Ars Poetica Juried Art/Poetry Show "where art and poetry meet" poems chosen to be illustrated by artists: 2019
- "Smokey Days and Nights" Photographer: Diane Hutchins, Bainbridge Public Library, Reading, March 1, 2019

Your Daily Poem Online
"Hardscrabble" September 12, 2019

Wording the Land Poetry Anthology, Port Townsend Market publication
"Hooray, Hooray, It's Market Day"
Reading at Market: December 21, 2019

2020
Ars Poetica Juried Art/Poetry Show "where art and poetry meet" poems chosen to be illustrated by artists: cancelled due to pandemic
- "I borrowed a walking stick" artist: Jacqueline Young
- "In My Garden" artist: Denise Cormier Mahoney
- "Winter Snow" artist: Spirit Bird Studio

The Leader Newspaper: Poetry Month
"I borrowed a walking stick"

Your Daily Poem Online
"Winter Snow" January 25
"Windstorm" April 14
"Dog and Squirrel" July 2

2021
Collective Visions Gallery Show, Bremerton, WA
"Winter Snow" Displayed with Print by
Harv Kolln Spirit Bird Studio

2022
Bainbridge Island Poetry Corners 2022 Competition, May Chap Book and Readings
"I borrowed a walking stick"
"April Snow"

2023

Ars Poetica Juried Art/Poetry Show "where art and poetry meet" poems chosen to be illustrated by artists:
- "Marching On" Photographer: Diane Hutchings
- "Windstorm" artist: Bob Rosenblat
- "Dog and Squirrel" artist: Irma Suplee

Your Daily Poem Online
"Hooray, Hooray, it's Market Day" March 6, 2023
"April Snow" April 21, 2023

Bainbridge Island Poetry Corners 2023 Competition: "Dog and Squirrel" Chap Book, Readings and Poster

a book of poetry

Judy Shimek Drechsler

Publishing Partners
2023

Publishing Partners
Marcia Breece
Port Townsend, WA 98368
www.marciabreece.com

Copyright © 2024 by Judy Drechsler

All rights reserved. No part of this book may be reproduced, stored in, or introduced into a retrieval system, or transmitted in any form, or by any means (electronic, mechanical, photocopying, recording, or otherwise) without the prior written permission of the publisher.

Printed in the United States of America

Library of Congress Control Number: 2024900038

ISBN: 978-1-944887-82-7

Cover design: Jane Jessen

In memory of my love, Mac Wheeler

And for my grandchildren, Jakob, James, Wyatt Jo and Charlotte

Contents

Poetry by Judy Shimek Drechsler iii
Foreword xiii
PART ONE: Mac 1
    When My Husband Died 3
    Cowgirl Skirts and Music Boxes 4
    Two Months After My Husband Died 6
    What Happened in the Woods 7
    My Old Friend Grief 8
    Widowhood 9
PART TWO: Survival 11
    Coronavirus Company 13
    Smokey Days and Nights 14
    Windstorm 15
    Winter Snow 16
    Dog and Squirrel 17
    I borrowed a walking stick 18
    Hardscrabble 20
    I Left the Dandelion Alone 21
    Marching On 22
PART THREE: Childhood Memories 23
    And What Would You Be Wanting Little Miss Judy? 25
    Summer Afternoons 26
    Improbable Respite 27
    My Mother's Jewelry Box 28
    The Twirler 29
    My Childhood Home, Red-tagged After 500 Year Flood 30
PART FOUR: Remembering 33
    April Snow 34
    In My Garden 35
    Hooray, Hooray, it's Market Day 36
    Dying is the Death of Distance 37
    walking in Nuremberg after a fall rain 38
    The Girls Sissu and Judy 39
    The Front Porch 40

PART FIVE: Family 41
    Chosen Sisters 43
    Turkey Notes 44
    Red Plastic Legos 46
    Two Heads on One Pillow 48
Publications and Presentations 51
Academic Awards 53
Gratitude 55
Author Bio 57

Foreword

We had twenty-six years together and they were years of adventures.

When my twenty-seven year old son heard I was going camping with a guy named Mac, he was a little worried. "Mom, camping, willingly? Who is this guy?" I was not known for my love of camping.

Mac introduced me to experiences I never would have done on my own. Buying an old wooden sailboat named Ginger and taking sailing lessons together. Camping in an old truck with an Alaskan camper on the back and a little metal plaque attached to rear fender that said, "It raises, it lowers".

He loved the back roads. As Wm. Least Heat Moon says in his book *Blue Highways* about the backroads of our nation, "Life doesn't happen on the interstate."

The first trip we took was to his favorite place in the world that we traveled back to many times in many campers...Lake Atlin in British Columbia. That was the first year we were together. That little camper had no bathroom, which meant I had to get up and walk a block in the dark, mosquito infested, woods if I needed one in the middle of the night. Obviously I was crazy in love with him that first year.

The second year I said, I'm still in love, I'm just not crazy anymore, and if I'm going to camp I want a camper with a bathroom in it. That was the first of many, many campers and camping trips.

He loved to read...mostly very, very long historical books about various wars and famous historical figures. He also loved poetry. One of the first things he bought me our first year together was a book of love poems that he would frequently read to me.

One of the many cards I received said it best:

Grief never ends...but it changes. It's a passage, not a place to stay.

Grief is not a sign of weakness, nor a lack of faith...it is the price of love.

There is no grief without a lot of joy first. I choose to remember the joy.

Part One
Mac

Hope smiles from the threshold of the year to come, whispering, "It will be happier."

— Alfred Tennyson

When My Husband Died
a villanelle 2017

Find joys in loss I say;
the stormy sky reflects my mood,
the edges of my mind foggy gray.

Bits of grief come together
to make a whole;
find joys in loss I say.

I listen to my memories
crowding into watery vision,
the edges of my mind foggy gray.

Thin slices of anxiety intrude.
What does the future hold now?
Find joys in loss I say,

There is no great grief
unless preceded by great joy;
the edges of my mind foggy gray.

I search my memories for
the stories of our life.
Find joys in loss I say,
the edges of my mind foggy gray.

Ars Poetica 2018, artist: Sarah June Steffen, Poulsbohemian Coffeehose

Cowgirl Skirts and Music Boxes
2017

One year he went back to
Maryland and brought me
back a circular cowgirl skirt
with gathers around the waist
that added at least
20 pounds to my frame
very thoughtful, but
I made him return it.

He made me laugh often,
one of the reasons I was attracted to him,
he always took my hand,
walking in the woods or
just down the street with the dog in tow,
one year I mentioned I loved music boxes
he bought me three
all of them played love songs.

Wandering off the main roads
resulted in grand adventures
and frequent irritation on my part,
getting lost in Provence,
discovering ruined castles
on hilltops in Germany,
exploring the back streets of Istanbul,
walking till dark looking for our hotel in France.

And the friends…oh the friends,
so many between the two of us,
now they all appear with flowers
and food and wonderful memories
they share with me,
kind words of sympathy flow
off their tongues in endless waves
drowning me in sorrow.

I'm feeling like I need to shed all
sympathy and smothering empathy
to experience true grief,
so I can let it go,
instead I clasp sadness close
over and over as each
loving friend hugs and
tries to protect me from it.

Oasis Journal 2018

Two Months After My Husband Died
2017

I crave the comfort of routine
rise at 7
read the paper
berries and bananas for breakfast
to the club for a workout
walk in the woods, rain or sun
lunch at Owl Sprit
take the dog to the beach
throw the ball over and over
home to watch the news
fish for dinner
bed by 9 to read

While I have an uncontrollable urge
to change things
rearrange furniture
clean out the closets
and cupboards
of things no longer needed
by one living alone
clothes no longer worn by
anyone living in this house
go out the door to Goodwill
the dog sleeps with me now.

What Happened in the Woods
2017

Emma, my dog

at home
with memories
of Mac
and sounds of
dying
in the woods

a hesitation

in his
step on the trail
Emma feels the
cascading wind
of the falling body

turns to look

rocks skidding
out from under foot
hands reaching
for ground

crack of skull

as it hits earth,
escaping last whoosh
of breath
like a wind
flowing through branches

ascending into the atmosphere

eagles fly
majestic wings spread

stillness

My Old Friend Grief
2021

In 2005,
when my 43 year old son was diagnosed with cancer,

I refused to let him in as Hope was my guest for many
months and there was no room for him.
When my son died, he pushed his way in the door

smashed and wrecked my house without apology.

I realized he had stood outside my door many times,
when my puppy died, hit by a bus, when my first husband
of 22 years left the family, when my mother passed away
of Alzheimer's...

mostly in the shadows and leaving quietly after hiding in
the bushes for a brief time, driven out
by Joy and Love who were
much preferred guests.

He returned in a surprise visit to my door five years ago
as a policeman calling to tell me my husband of 26 years
had died while walking the dog in the woods.

This time I let him in the first time he knocked, offered
him tea, realizing it was useless to lock the door
and pretend he wasn't there,
but I hired Busyness to distract me.

He kept me company constantly that first year,
but stayed away longer and longer when he realized
Joy and Love were often
staying in my guest bedroom,
though he returned whenever they went home,

like longtime friends you really don't enjoy having
around, but endure because they are irretrievably
part of your life now.

I'm fixing another room just for him,
because I know he'll be back.

Widowhood
2021

Time stumbles on like a
poorly trained marching band
after your designation
changes to widow,

the rhythm of life
without a spouse
becomes a winding road
surprises around each bend.

Seven more friends took on the
black mantle of widowhood this year,
we gather for tea and tears,
in days of unbearable sadness.

No beauty or comfort in this word.
Etymology: 15th century Old English, widowe
Empty, destitute, bereft,
Designation of a solitary sadness,

we become the background without a spouse.
It grieves me to think of you in the past;
kissing the joy of those years as they fly away*,
many things I still have yet to do.

*Eternity *by William Blake*

Part Two
Survival

The birds they sang at the break of day,
Start again, I heard them say.
Don't dwell on what has passed away,
Ring the bells that still can ring,
Forget your perfect offering.
There is a crack in everything,
That's how the light gets in.

— Leonard Cohen

Coronavirus Company
2020

Amos Ant, the scout came first marching across the rusty
orange granite pattern of my countertop,
foraging for crumbs from cookies baked
yesterday, leaving his scent trail like
Hansel and Gretel so he
could find his way back home.

Fred Fly flew in one day, despite most
flights being cancelled, taking a leisurely walk
on my clean vertical windowpanes, hanging
upside down on my 12' ceiling, moving from wall to
coffee table and a leftover piece of apple while he
waited for a flight out and back home.

Behind my dining room chest Sally Spider
had constructed a large home in the hopes
of inviting her own guests for dinner.
Her cupboard was empty, so I released
her onto my Hydrangea bush, where
she could more easily fill her pantry.

Jim Junco came looking for love the last three days,
throwing himself at my car's side mirror
hoping for an amoure with the beautiful bird
who lived there. No matter how long
he persisted she did not find him attractive; he did
no better with the one in the mirror on the other side.

Company is where you find it, especially now....

Smokey Days and Nights
2019

Like a gray broody hen
settling her feathers on the nest,
smoke falls softly into Port Townsend Bay,
covering the blue water in gray swirls, slowly
erasing the scenic mountain grandeur.

The faces of fire are many, a cheery campfire,
sparks filling the air, comfort of heat on cold hands,
a glass of wine on the couch in front of a
crackling fire in the living room grate while snow
drifts gently past the window.

But these new fires are passionate as an ardent lover,
all consuming, leaping from tree to tree in violent,
twirling tornados of flame, creating new landscapes,
turning woods to piles of ash, homes to black foundations,
reducing lives to the minimal needs of a newborn babe.

Ars Poetica 2019, Photographer: Diane Hutchins

Windstorm
2020

gusts grab the tree tops
of the giant Doug Fir
heave them towards the sky
snakes around the Red Cedar
howling and snapping branches

recklessly flinging garbage cans
down the driveway
lifting lawn chairs
effortlessly
into the agitated air

turning the
waltzing rhythm
of the tree line
into rock and roll
dancing

frantic wind-shredded clouds
throw tantrums of
epic proportions
run madly to the South
escaping into the distant horizon

the whirling wind
chases after
nipping at the tail
of the racing darkness

Your Daily Poem Online, April 14, 2020
Ars Poetica 2023, artist: Bob Rosenblat

Winter Snow
2019

everything's a cupcake
perched on a freshly ironed white sheet,
white frosting spread in swirls on

peaked copper roof of my
restaurant for birds,

bare hydrangea branches
cozily wrapped in white ermine,

ferns bowed down,
on the white plate of earth,

bird bath now an ice-skating rink,
all crisp and clean

until I let the dog out

Published Collective Visions Gallery Show, Bremerton, WA
Displayed with Print by Harv Kolin, Spirit Bird Studio, 2021
Your Daily Poem Online, January 25, 2020

Dog and Squirrel
2020

Ears laid back.
Rigid legs shiver with rage.
Mad whines split the air.
Nose pressed against glass.

Twitching nose.
Swishing brown tail.
Feet clutch top of wood fence
ready to sprint.

Door ajar.
Dog leaps out.
With wild barking
claws at fence,
runs back and forth.

Squirrel streaks along fence top.
Leaps into the gnarled pear tree,
onto the top of the pergola.
Darts to the giant red cedar,
disappears into leafy hideaway
he calls home.

Dog whines,
settles in to wait.
Forever patient,
squirrel chatters
his displeasure...
or maybe he's laughing.

Your Daily Poem Online, July 2, 2020
Bainbridge Island Poetry Corners 2023 Competition
Ars Poetica 2023, artists: Irma Suplee

I BORROWED A WALKING STICK
2019

from the forest
mossy bark, her dress
the forest didn't mind

Walking slowly I bend down
an oval, mottled brown and black rock
will live on my kitchen windowsill
memories of my forest visit

My eyes close,
smell and hearing open their doors wide
chee, chee, chee slides down my ear canals
a bird tells the story of her day
moisture laden air invades my nostrils

I glance at the water plants
their long slender stems and leaves
shuddering gently
in a stealthy breeze

Rough bark peels off my stick as
my hand grips it,
three yellow Birch leaves cling
stubbornly to a tree otherwise winter naked
waiting for spring

Hanging moss, dressing the trees for winter
skeletons of Elm and Birch
double their size in perfect pond reflections

Drizzle turns into
white balls making random designs
on black yoga pants

Charred wood like black soil,
in the fire pit, giving its life to provide warmth,
white balls of ice fill up its black, shiny cracks,
all things in nature get along

Brown ferns crunch under foot
life and death live side by side
small rock warm in my pocket
I return my walking stick to its forest home
the perfect guest.

The Port Townsend Leader Newspaper: *Poetry Month, April 2020*
Ari Poetica 2020 artist: Jacqueline Young,
Bainbridge Island Poetry Corner 2022 Compition

HARDSCRABBLE
2019

Sarcastic lacy branches drenched in heat
produce inferior vegetation,

impoverished brown leaves desiccated and
wrinkled before their time survive by
curling into a crevice waiting for rain,

cotyledons die before their stored
nutrition can nurture new leaves.

There is a beauty in this misery,

dry brown twigs dance in silvery dust
blown below wind shredded clouds,

fragile beauty survives in simplicity and
lack of ornamentation,

life trickles up stems and trunks
exhausted but determined.

Your Daily Poem Online, September 2019
The Port Townsend Leader Newspaper, *April 2020, National Poetry*

I Left the Dandelion Alone
2022

After years of energetically
pulling and digging
the butter yellow weed
relegating it to the yard waste
with the crab grass and thistles,

I left this one alone

After hearing about the distress
of deserted beehives
destroyed by careless use of pesticides,
and a new threat of Murder Hornets
slaughtering whole hives,

I left this one alone

After reading a quote from
Einstein that predicted if
bees become extinct
humans will have only
4 years to live,

I left this one alone

After learning bees and other
pollinators use the flowers as
their first bit of sustenance
after emerging from
a winter of hibernation,

I left this one alone

to feed that first bee as it
opens its wings to the warm
sun of spring and, full of hope,
seeks that first meal of
pollen and nectar,

I left this one alone

Marching On
2021

Over the still cold world a bird sings a mournful note,
like a protected heart, the blood red flower

of my wild rose
begins to open on the lowest branch.

Tulips burst through the dead ground hungry for sunshine,
brave daffodils, tall soldiers, unfurl their golden trumpets

as though announcing spring is just down that
winter road still frosty in the early morning.

Hyacinths, pansies, primroses, a virtual rainbow
shining through the chilly rain and anemic sunbeams.

A parade of fat buds marching over the rhododendron bushes
ready to explode into vibrant reds and pinks at the first hint of warmth.

A breeze caresses my cheek as I take my walk
I like to think it's my late husband letting me know that life continues.

Ars Poetica 2023, Photographer: Diane Hutchings

Part Three
Childhood Memories

Everything else you grow out of,
but you never recover from childhood.

— Beryl Bainbridge

And What Would You Be Wanting Little Miss Judy?
2018

Half a block down and across the street from
childhood the tiny store rises from an uneven sidewalk
the screen door ripping gracefully
from its wooden frame three steps up.

I open it to the scent of apples in a barrel, dill from a pickle
crock, cool waves of air escaping from the meat counter
where Mrs. Nelson pulls out 6 hot dogs strung together,
wraps them in white paper for the lady in the flowered house
dress with a grocery bag hanging loosely from her hand.

I pause at the cloudy glass counter where Smith Brother's
licorice whips fill a see-through glass, needles and threads
line up in colorful abundance, sharpened
Ticonderoga pencils are sun beams in a jar.
Bit O'Honey, Bubble Gum Cigars, Candy Buttons and
Cigarettes, Jujubes, Red Hots, O Henry bars –
my mouth can still taste the sweetness.

Mrs. Nelson's spotted white apron lies around her ample hips,
her dark hair is streaked with gray and pinned up on one side,
curled girlishly around her chubby cheeks.
With a pudgy finger,
she pushes the correct button. I hear the clang of the brass
cash register, see her give its crank her signature enthusiastic
turn, know my memories are no small purchase.

Summer Afternoons
2019

Mrs. Simon hangs out a pair of long
red underwear. The legs stream out
horizontally in a spring breeze.

Mother appears at the screen door,
waves to the mailman, hurries down the walk
to see what news he has brought.

In the alley an old yellow cat searches for lunch
and peanut butter on my tongue urges me forward
up the skinny Japanese elm branches,
higher into my leafy hideaway.

Improbable Respite
2020

musty cabin in rustic
wilds of Minnesota
smells like damp blankets

through dirty glass of small window
murky lake reflects moist heat waves rising
into gnat filled air

small spider spins enormous web in
corner of ceiling
flies rolled up and stashed in his pantry

dust motes sail across the room
in a streak of sunlight
covers creaky floorboards

mother frowns
brushes cobwebs from her face
reaches for a broom

my 8 year old self knows
she is not happy, this is my
father's idea of downtime

My Mother's Jewelry Box
2015

The bedroom door opens with a faint creak
loud in the empty house.
After school I am home alone for a few hours
only my Cocker Spaniel for company.

The sun is low in the sky
casting a shadowy film over the
dresser that holds my
Mother's jewelry box.

In the quiet I make my way across the
room and slowly open the
black box with roses carved on its lid.
My Mother's jewels shine out like a sunny day.

Large earrings shaped like white daisies
that cover my 10 year old ears.
A long necklace of pearls, real I'm sure,
wraps around my neck twice.

A blue, sparkly broach I pin
to my Red Rider sweat shirt,
stands out like a blue spotlight
on the bright yellow background.

The "diamond" bracelet slips onto my tiny wrist
and stays on only if I keep my arm extended upward,
the better to admire its elegance.

Rings of all hues slide around my small fingers
sparkling in the late afternoon sunshine.

I am beautiful.

The Twirler
2020

At eight I got my first baton.

At twelve I twirled it to Yellow Rose of Texas
in the sixth grade talent show.

At 15 I made the twirling team in high school
high stepping it before 60 boys and girls
playing musical instruments.
Early morning practices,
7 am in the neighborhood
surrounding Jefferson High School.

Parades in Cedar Rapids
and the towns surrounding it.
Marching down streets lined with people,
short skirt swishing, brass buttons shining,
white boots with swinging tassels,
a tall hat strapped under my chin.
Mom worked on the fourth floor of a downtown building.
She leaned out the window to wave at me.

By 17 I was at the head of the band,
huge blue and white feathered hat,
large impressive baton keeping rhythm.
I can feel the soft green turf under my boots
as I strut down the football field
toward the goal posts,
loud band behind me,
cheering and yelling in the stands.

I love marching songs.
My knees lift and toes point down
when I hear one.
Mother used to sing behind her walker.
I will march.

My Childhood Home, Red-tagged After 500 Year Flood of Cedar River
2015

The river flowed through my life,
lapping the sides of the old rowboat,
grandpa and I,
our fishing lines riding up
and down small hills of waves.

Fishing with Walt,
the neighbor boy,
sitting companionably on the
edge of the shore, bare feet,
cold mud between our toes,

Diana, JoAnn and I
run across the creaky,
1888 Railroad Bridge
peeking between the spaces of the
metal grid into the whirling depths.

River Road followed the curves
of our waterway to downtown,
lined with small, modest homes.
I often walked the levee,
boundary between river and road.

Only one disturbing
memory tucked away
in my mind, pulsing, spinning
water overflowing the levies
one spring weekend,

pawing the big wooden fence
supported with sand bags,
rising across the street, me home
from college, sleeping in my clothes,
ready for the order to evacuate.

Nearly a half century later,
a 500-year flood turned the
Cedar River into a raging torrent
tearing through large
sections of the city,

covering that little house
I grew up in to the rooftop
angrily stirring the belongings
into a riotous disarray,
impossible to recognize or clean up.

Today a green wavy meadow remains,
dandelion fluff spinning in the wind
taking my heart away,
all gone.

Part Four
Remembering

Life is available only in the present moment.
— Thich Nhat Hanh

You are the sky. Everything else is just the weather.
— Pema Chodra

April Snow
2021

Tiny pear blossom petals
slide down the runways of gentle breezes

not particular where they land,

decorating my hair like pearls,
tickling my face,

covering the brick patio
like a warm white blanket.

Leaving small green pears exposed,
so the sun can fold itself gently around them,

urging them to yellow ripeness.

Thousands of tiny sails,
letting go of beautiful puffy white snowballs

that clothe the ancient orchard tree

in my yard.

Bainbridge Island Poetry Corners Compition, 2022
Your Daily Poem Online, April 21, 2023

In My Garden
2020

Pink sunburn
kissed by the sun
feathery petals
eiderdown beds for ants
Peonies

Perpetually cheery
smiles on heads
pointed upwards
he loves me, he loves me not
Daisys

Purple waterfalls
cascading
smelling of memories
Great Grandmother's yard
Lilacs

Plump balls of color
blue, white, pink, green
beautiful in
dried death
Hydrangeas

Blinding yellow
black seedy center
raises its broad face to the sky
reaches for warm rays
Sunflowers

A lesson in survival
yellow heads become gray
uses wind to create a vortex
swirling long distances
Dandelions

Ars Poetica 2020, artist: Denise Cormier Mahoney

Hooray, Hooray, it's Market Day
2019

Peaked white roofs point towards the rising sun.
Market day in Port Townsend! I walk up the street,
basket swinging from my hand.
The buzz of small town conversations reach me first,
the music of guitar and keyboard bounce into my ears.

Vendor carts filled with beauty from local organic farms
line both sides of the street, march down the middle.
A riotous disarray of smells baking bread, grilled salmon,
bratwurst. A delicate lust makes me
buy more than I can possibly eat.

Cheeses, tasty award winners, sit on crispy crackers.
Purple Lilacs, red and yellow Dahlias, frilled pink tulips,
soy candles with appealing names, Eggplant, Heirloom
Tomato, Cinderella Pumpkin, Lemon Basil, all
eager to light the way to my evening dinner table.

Golden, deep green, and brilliant orange squash of all
shapes spill out from baskets and boxes.
Beans abound, purple, yellow, white and green, lay in untidy
   heaps,
flanked by crisp green and white striped zucchini and juicy
tomatoes in an array of yellows and reds.

In my mind I see them sitting on my kitchen counter,
as much at home in the stillness of my kitchen as at the busy
   market.
My dinner plate waits patiently for their goodness.

Wording the Land Poetry Collection 2019 *Jefferson County Farmers
Markets Port Townsend, WA*
Your Daily Poem Online, March 6, 2023

Dying is the Death of Distance
2019

Italy Day 3
foggy morning lake front,
stepping gingerly over
rough, uneven stones,
a steadying hand takes mine,
spangles of sunlight
reflected on the waves
sprinkle the edges of my eyesight,
he is always with me now

mind filled with backroad
images traveled,
blue lines on the map,
going nowhere,
going everywhere,
his deep, humorous voice
encouraging me to explore
places I would never have
thought of going
on my own

WALKING IN NUREMBERG AFTER A FALL RAIN
2016

fall soup of golds, reds and oranges,
dead leaves seek the ground,

softly caressing the small plaques of souls gone,
embedded in the walkway,

wind wanders, as if lost, through the branches
standing naked and exposed to the moving air

wrinkled, faded, crisp, they drop from the branches
balance like gliders on the currents of cold air

landing in puddles reflecting gray sky
cracking the picture of the world into pieces

hundreds of black dots move across the puddles
flapping synchronicitous wings, V shapes pointing south

Ars Poetica 2018, artist: Joanne Schoener Scott Front Street Gallery

The Girls Sissu and Judy
2009

Where are the girls
of 50 years ago,
who laughed and talked
and drank Coca Cola
in the summer of '59?

Strangers, until that
American Field Service
Summer, entwined
our lives with a
string of memories.

The heat of the Sauna,
chill of the lake,
buying fresh milk from
the farm next door,
riding the street cars to town.

Tossing pitchforks of hay onto
tall stacks, our hair tied back
with cotton scarves. Riding the
motor boat with the wind in our
laughing faces. Life ahead of us.

The Front Porch
2018

Tony was dead,
hit by a bus.
His small puppy body taken away,
buried in the back yard. I was 5.
I sat on the second step
on the small front porch and cried.
Mom gave me a bottle of Coca Cola

Mom stormed out and disappeared for the day.
I was going to Shirley Meeker's 8th birthday party.
I sat on the front porch in my party clothes,
tears rolling down my cheeks.
"It'll be okay," said Dad, "she'll be back,"

A For Sale sign in front of the little bungalow.
At ten it was the only home I had ever known.
I sat on the front porch and read my comic books,
a few carefully hung over the For Sale sign.

Christmas time, snow and ice
shoveled clear so I could sit on the top step,
wait for the Christmas mail,
some days, two deliveries,
enjoyable anticipation of
many letters and cards to open.

Early adolescence returning from
playing pool at the Y, a block away,
after dark, porch light always a
narrow, shining path down to the street,
illuminating that little front porch,
calling me home.

Part Five
Family

then joining hands to ...hands
would bid them cling together,
for there is no friend like a sister
in calm or stormy weather,
to cheer one on the tedious way,
to fetch one if one goes astray,
to lift one if one totters down,
to strenghten whilst one stands.

—From *Goblin Market* by Christina Rossetti

CHOSEN SISTERS
2023

Jane came first
all blonde hair and
full of sass and confidence.

Then Bernie snared my son
who noticed her changing into
work shoes at the desk
next to his the first day of his new job.

Heather blew into our lives
like a wild wind, a cheeky 11 year old,
who, eventually, fit right into this
little group of beautiful, smart,
confident girls that make up my life.

All sisters now, love strung out over the years
and many weekends of togetherness and fun.

Turkey Notes
2022

*"Turkey Green,
Turkey yellow,*

Holiday meals fill a
special space in the mind,
traditions abound,
special ways of setting the table,
Turkey Notes at each place,
written by the youngest.

*Turkey is a very
Fine fellow."*

Special dishes served
so often it seems sac religious to have
turkey without Great Grandma's
special sauerkraut, or
Christmas breakfast without
poppy seed coffee cake
from the local Czech bakery.

*"Turkey purple,
Turkey white,*

What makes one
holiday meal take root
in our minds forever?

*Turkey says,
Take a bite."*

The Thanksgiving my first Grandson
sat at the table with us in a "real" chair,
a plateful of applesauce
perched in front of him.
As we all dug into turkey, sauerkraut,
mashed potatoes, cranberry sauce and hot rolls
he exclaimed in a loud voice as he
scooped up big spoonfuls of applesauce,
"This is the best Thanksgiving dinner I've ever had!"

"Turkey red,
Turkey blue,

The first holiday without my son alive
his empty chair at the full table,
grief still fresh and stunning,
disbelief writ large in all our minds,
fueling a new urgency to keep
connections and love
strong between us.

Turkey says,
I love you!"

Red Plastic Legos
2017

For my grandson Jakob, on the occasion of his high school graduation

Light glows through
red plastic Legos
joined in the shape
of a heart balanced
on its narrowest point,
a love gift
for grandma.

Images of the baby
he used to be,
pushing off on
one leg to
crawl faster,
as a toddler he
loved to run

down the mall,
arms and legs
pumping until
his face turned red,
grandma close on
his heels
trying to catch up.

Eight year old fingers
shaped a warship of 1500 Legos
in half the time directions
said it should take,
at 6 he arranged
dinosaurs on the stairs
in order of geologic period.

Those fingers now
strum guitar strings,
bounce basketballs,
do pull ups
on the bar in the
the frame of
the doorway,

rest casually on
the steering wheel
as he drives
to school, contemplating
college next year
with the confidence
felt at 17.

Grandma watches
from the
background
of his life,
in admiration,
the young man
he's become.

Two Heads on One Pillow
2020

*To my grandson James, on the occasion of
his high school graduation*

I miss the simple, innocent days of
piano recitals, whirlwind hugs
when I arrived for a visit,

conversations and massages
before bedtime
when I stayed over,

slept in his room
small head close to mine,
explosion of soft blond curls,
pug nose searching for its shape

we talked of seals and zombies,
the bunny club he started in 2nd grade,
no rules, just had to like bunnies,

this is the life, he would sigh,
no school for two days,
basketball tomorrow,
grandma giving me a massage,

while we have conversations

lined up on a shelf,
trophies tell of a love of movement
soccer, basketball, baseball

now he steps onto the road of life,
friends surrounding him as he heads
towards college and career
now he holds another woman's hand

blonde curls dancing in the breeze,
walks with her, different conversations

now he drives confidently
looks for a job,
moving towards independence

grandma backs away, but stays
close enough so they
still have conversations

Publications and Presentations

Drechsler, J. (1993). *No More Spelling Tests! Learning to Spell in a Whole Language Classroom Teacher's Networking Whole Language Newsletter,* Richard C. Owens Publishers, Inc. NYC

Drechsler, J. (1992). Student Self Evaluation & Fast-Write Evaluation Exercise.

The Whole Language Catalog supplement on Authentic Assessment, (96 & 165) American School Publishers, K. Goodman, Y. Goodman and L. Bridges Bird. (contributing author articles)

Drechsler, J. (1991). *Spelling In A Whole Language Classroom.* Classroom Based Research of a Whole Language Spelling Program, *Alaska Teacher Researcher Network Publication* (journal article)

Drechsler, J. (1989). A Whole Language Classroom. *Alaska Council of Teachers of English and Alaska State Reading Association Journal.* (journal article)

Self-published for University Classes:
Drechsler, J. & P. Lloyd, *Let Them Write! A Guide to Primary and Intermediate Writing Workshop*

ACADEMIC AWARDS

Awarded City University's President's Distinguished Instructor Award for 2004.

Nominated BP Teacher of Excellence 1998 by parents at Polaris K-12 Alternative School

Special Appointment as Anchorage School District Teacher-in-Residence, University of Alaska Anchorage School of Education 1991-92.

Recipient, University of Alaska Anchorage Kappa Delta Pi Student Honor Society, Excellence in Teaching Award, given by students, March, 1992.

Finalist, Anchorage Education Association Teacher of the Year, 1987.

Gratitude

This book would not have been possible without the nurturing encouragement of my longtime writing teacher and friend, Sheila Bender, who has led me through the maze of creating poetic thought and expression over the last fifteen years.

Thanks to my daughter, Jane Jessen, who designed the cover for the book and to Marcia Breece who helped this book materialize.

Also a big thank you to all the poetry competitions, especially Ars Poetica and Bainbridge Island Poetry Corners, who magically reappeared after three years of COVID and gave Northwest poets places to spread their wings and put their poetry into the public arena once again.

My family and friends are the inspiration for most of my creations and I am forever grateful to all of them.

AUTHOR BIO
Teacher, Poet, Writer

*J*udy spent most of her teaching career in Anchorage, Alaska where she taught Reading Methods, Language Arts and Children's Literature, Writing Workshops and Miscue Analysis in graduate and undergraduate courses for the University of Alaska Anchorage as well as being a full-time primary teacher in the Anchorage School District.

Her last two years in Alaska were spent as a Reading/Writing Workshop consultant for the Anchorage School District and as a Writing Workshop consultant for other school districts throughout Alaska where she conducted teacher training and workshops for various districts. She served as President of the Alaska State Literacy Association and was a member of the Alaska Department of Education Curriculum Cabinet.

Since retirement from the Anchorage School District and the University of Alaska and moving to Washington State, she has taught for Seattle City University's Master's Degree in Teaching, BA in Education, and Distance Learning programs serving as instructor for the Reading and Language Arts courses. Serving as a mentor for teachers implementing Writing Workshops into their curriculum here on the Peninsula and in Redmond has kept her in Elementary and Junior High classrooms.

www.ingramcontent.com/pod-product-compliance
Lightning Source LLC
Chambersburg PA
CBHW050044080526
44586CB00014B/1448